BANTUSTAN BLUES

TJIZEMBUA TJIKUZU

Published by Akashic Books

ISBN: 978-1-63614-246-3

Printed in China
First printing

EU Authorized Representative details:
Easy Access System Europe
Mustamäe tee 50, 10621 Tallinn, Estonia
gpsr.request@easproject.com

Akashic Books
Instagram, X, Facebook: AkashicBooks
info@akashicbooks.com
www.akashicbooks.com

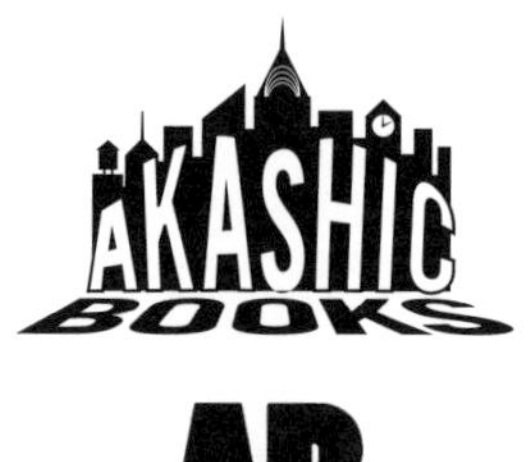

African Poetry Book Fund
Brown University
10 Prospect Street
Box A
Providence, RI 02912

TABLE OF CONTENTS

PREFACE

by Henk Rossouw

Tjizembua Tjikuzu's *Bantustan Blues* asks what "home" means in the aftermath. What sense of home remained after the colonial German campaign of genocide, largely against the Herero people, during the early twentieth century in what was then called German South West Africa? Or after South Africa declared a Bantustan around Aminuis, the speaker's birthplace, and continued its apartheid policies, its structural violence against the Black majority in Namibia, until the early 1990s? "The Timbuktu blues of twilight are not a shield against the rupturing shock waves of history," Tjikuzu writes in the title poem of this searing, brilliant chapbook. "If the dead do speak in blues, what are they saying? / Do they wish to comfort us?" ("Bantustan Blues").

On the night the poem begins, the dead are cold comfort: "The night spreads over the expansive savanna like soot on leaves after a bushfire. / Mother is at the sugar doctor's in Windhoek. Grandparents are all dead and buried." Yet the love that Tjikuzu's speaker feels for home, and for the people, living and dead, who tie him to home, contradicts history—perhaps in the same way that a pebble contradicts a bulldozer with its refusal to be destroyed. In Tjikuzu's poetry, that refusal can take the form of a praise song, where "what is left" can be renewed by the memory of the speaker's mother: "Home is my mother by the fire, humming what is left of her matrilineal praise song / while she stirs pumpkin soup in a three-legged cauldron" ("Bantustan Blues"). Declarative, rhythmic, detail-rich lines like these abound in *Bantustan Blues.*

On a deeper level, Tjikuzu's work seeks to restore that which whiteness—in the shape of German imperialism, South African colonization, and ongoing racism—has sought to destroy. For Tjikuzu, images of home, as they relate to land or people, are acts of political reclamation. At the same time, he utilizes simplicity: "Mother is at the sugar doctor's in Windhoek" underscores the gulf the speaker feels between Aminuis, on the eastern edge of Namibia, and the distant capital city. And there's the striking diction of "sugar doctor's," containing in its resonance the toll of diabetes on the human body, as well as the suggestion of a sugar pill, a placebo—of continual visits to the city that don't help.

These ambiguities in *Bantustan Blues* create a poetic environment in which even "a bad omen" is a welcome sign of the home ground where Tjikuzu's speaker belongs: "Home is a white-faced owl sitting on the tree, hooting a bad omen / with her curved beak" ("Bantustan Blues"). The vivid image of the "white-faced owl" in the first poem is a foretaste of the animal poems that follow. Refreshingly, the borders of Tjikuzu's consideration are open to the non-human world, which the poet explores with empathy and imagination. "*Archispirostreptus gigas*" is a gorgeous address to a multitude of millipedes, "even sneaking into the layers of my grandmother's petticoats," whose arrival in a dry country signals rain and longed-for renewal:

> because when you came,
> feeling the rough skins of our dung huts
> with your fickle antennae,
> I knew the waiting was over.

Motifs of rings and cycles recur in "*Archispirostreptus gigas*," forming a poignant meditation on the evolutionary laws of birth, mortality, succession, and rebirth—laws that both humans and millipedes obey.

Similarly, the blunt grief for a long-dead animal in "Dog Ode" develops into a plea against time, with the dog still momentarily alive in the present tense of the poem. This is a plea that the lyric poem achieves at its best; Tjikuzu employs the full power of the form. "Dog Ode" exemplifies what American poet and critic Susan Stewart calls "that art of felt thought":

I have made the same mistake again,
missing you into existence,
the fool that I am,
while I have you in a place
where death can't reach you.

Maybe what home means, in Tjikuzu's gifted hands, is not only to sing of the living, but also to bring back the dead for a moment, for the brief window of time the lyric opens.

Whether writing from the perspective of Sudan, the last male northern white rhinoceros, or addressing a deceased relative, Tjikuzu's empathy as an artist constitutes a valuing of every living thing, past and present, human and non-human alike. "Home," then, is a fierce, ongoing project, a place to be restored both internally and politically in the aftermath of Namibia's history. In *Bantustan Blues*, Tjikuzu offers us imagery that blurs the line between the living and dead, between memory and aftermath. "Portrait of My Grandfather" demonstrates this tension between presence and mortality, with its indelible image of "a long club of a mopane tree held lightly in your right hand / as though to write in the sand." Yes, Tjikuzu's poetry is truly striking.

BANTUSTAN BLUES

The night spreads over the expansive savanna like soot on leaves after a bushfire.
Mother is at the sugar doctor's in Windhoek. Grandparents are all dead and buried.
There is no adult at home, except my fifteen-year-old brother, to ease the teeth of the impending night.

Even with the fire burning, warming our hands, and *Kanuamaihi* and Orion hanging above us
like beacons of hope—how sure I am, of the strong pull at that part of me I cannot touch or
pin down—dread—as if my soul is standing on a high desert mesa,
an omnipotent voice daring me to jump into the sea of dunes below.

Reservation dogs howl like cunning jackals caught in a trap when they feel that chill blow.

The Timbuktu blues of twilight are not a shield against the rupturing shock waves of history.

*

If the dead do speak in blues, what are they saying?
Do they wish to comfort us?
If I stare into the twilight long enough, will my dirge turn into a joyous rhapsody?
Is blue the love of ancestors reflected back to us?
If twilight sings, why does my heart droop
like a foxglove heavy with rainwater?
Why this harrowing? Why this howling?

*

Home is a white-faced owl sitting on the tree, hooting a bad omen
with her curved beak.

Home is my mother by the fire, humming what is left of her matrilineal praise song
while she stirs pumpkin soup in a three-legged cauldron.

Home is a place I am eager to return to—but not without an unexplainable
dread that puffs up
at the pit of my stomach as if I have grown a second heart.

Home is a vertigo of landscapes and emotions coagulating like a bale of tumble-
weeds
in the wind.

NAMES AND WARNINGS

After Lothar von Trotha's extermination order,
after the blood of Herero women and children had soaked
and bespoiled the leaves of the sacred shepherd's tree
where young men slaughtered Nguni heifers
and fed the holy ground with fresh blood
and contents of the ruminant gut,
the names of Herero children changed
from *Ndundumehi, Karungukongue*—
names immovable as mountains in the earth,
as certain as the great paws of a male leopard
striking the red sands—
to accusatory and abstracted names
like *Tjiṱa, Tjizembua, Periua, Pepua*—
names that hint at the unutterable
like the dent of a bullet
lodged in the muscular flesh of the heart.

As the years come and go,
it all begins to make sense—
why elders sneered and scolded our uncorrupted innocence
with names like *Kuraumune,*
grow up and see,
a warning like cotton-muffled thunder
from a toothless and reeking mouth that gave
no rancid word as bread to a sapling soul.

ARCHISPIROSTREPTUS GIGAS

Before and after Sir Roger Penrose's conformal cyclic cosmology.

If they were to ask me
where you stashed your eggs, Prince of Rain,
I wouldn't know. But you always did
come—uninvited yet purposeful, gliding across the sands
with your myriad legs. And like your legs,
you numbered by the thousands: coiling around
legs of three-legged cauldrons, coiling under
water buckets and baskets of maize, sliding into cavities
in firewood where the marrow used to be,
and even sneaking into the layers of my grandmother's petticoats.
In those years, I revered you, Prince of Rain,
because when you came,
feeling the rough skins of our dung huts
with your fickle antennae,
I knew the waiting was over.
We could finally release the sighs
we had been holding since Witvlei's cold breath
blew over and licked the green grass
with its white tongue of death.
And when it poured, you were drowned
in that very thing that called you to life again
and your skeletons were left scattered
under an assertive sun.
But you should know how,
called by your lustrous rain-scented bones,
we pulled apart your segmented bodies
and wore your rings on our ring fingers—
with the luster of that sable chitin

against our sable skin,
we became the adults we couldn't wait to be.
But even with your skeletons squandered,
intestines devoured by red ants and toothed zephyr,
I never despaired, because I knew
that somewhere, a new generation of your kind was preparing
for a chance at this seemingly purposeless succession
that we all must partake in.

JUNE BUGS

In January we sail kites, feasting on the camel thorn bush
breaking into bloom outside our grandparents' yard.
After a large bowl of omaere and pap,
my brothers and I raid the bush,
yanking out dark-green June bugs with bold cream lines
bordering their exoskeletons, or leaf green
with white spots on their abdomens, or dull brown
with broad shells and strong joints, or rare light brown
with tiny black spots from thorax to elytra.
We find them grinding the bush's branches,
bleeding out the stems with their diligent mandibles.
We each pluck one from the nest,
clasp them in our small hands, their serrated
legs grazing against our sweaty palms
as they lumber to crawl out—
their tiny compound eyes and antennae cowering
under the soft taut flesh of our palms.
Using our grandmother's sewing thread,
we take a long thread and make a knot at its end
with a hole wide enough for a June bug's hind leg,
then tie two or three knots, tethering the kite,
so it won't escape.
We like the bulky, dull brown ones with strong joints best;
their legs never separate from their abdomen,
even when we yank the line.
We fly them for hours—their wings
droning hard to reach the unreachable.
Giving them the thread, the false freedom,
then reeling them in again,

holding them at arm's length
to better hear the music of their labor.
Our faces beam with delight:
eyes squinting to avoid the Kalahari sun,
nostrils flaring as we work the thread,
mouths curling in everlasting giggles
as if we are watching a funny puppet show.
At the end of playtime, we feed the dead to chickens and sand,
free those that can still fly,
and return the broken-legged, broken-winged
to the nest for more sugar and water—
our hands bug shit–stained and loud with sap.

DOG ODE

Today, I remembered you
differently. Not like I always do,
a spade beating out what is left
in your collapsed lungs—
an act of mercy.

Today, I remembered your milk-white fur,
and the twin mountain ridges
that ran across your back—traces
of a Hottentot hunting dog ancestor—
the ridges in which your fury resided.

But now that you are here,
I have made the same mistake again,
missing you into existence,
the fool that I am,
while I have you in a place
where death can't reach you.

WINDELINE

Red purse.
    Worn-out red leather purse.
    Golden eagle dollar
in withered hands.

I cannot place your face
exactly.

Lady of toenails coiling
like the horns of a mountain goat;

I have your marks in me.

Your voice? All
gone now, muted like dry leaves
buried under
a sleeping puff adder.

In the chaotic mornings of our kicks and wails,
your walking stick stings like a desert scorpion
on our clean-shaven heads.

Red purse
    in brown weathered hands.
Your golden dollar feeds me.
Feeds me like bread.
More than bread.

Grandmother, red lady.
Red lady of warring bloods.

It is you I come to for courage in the dark.

You lady of heavy winds and spirits.
You lady of fermented peas and hymns.

When the mountains close in,
I whisper your forbidden name
into the hungry wind:
~~Kauniva~~, ~~Kauniva~~, ~~Kauniva~~.
And the night parts in threes.

PORTRAIT OF MY GRANDFATHER

I remember you like this:
seated in your chipped white chair,
woolly black hair and beard with patches of white,
dressed in your gray preaching suit,
a long club of a mopane tree held lightly in your right hand
as though to write in the sand.
There was also your abandoned white '57 Ford sedan
thrown on its back, a secondhand
relic from a time before our birth—
young sisters' eyes peeled
to the two-tracked road,
waiting for their father's Ford sedan
to arrive from Boer Farms beyond
the reservations.
I remember the desert gardens
of wild cucumbers, gourds, and melons
you tended with care,
like a gateway to an Eden
that was to be our inheritance.
On your date of death,
you dressed in white like the angels
of your god above
and sauntered, cool-footed, without protest,
into the beguiling light of the sunset.
On the weekend of your burial,
I will forever remember the contralto weeper
who knew your people;
how she floated out of that Toyota bakkie
like a giant multicolored octopus disembarking a ship,

how her shattered voice trembled in the radiating air,
how she arrested our hearts with her praise song
and gave our sorrow true tone—
praising the women who carried you,
naming the women who bore you—
Ovakuendata vo yaRupju—
making her way to the tabernacle of weepers,
the song splattering in her throat
as if she is distilling tears
into nourishing rain.

BAPTISM AT SEA

Unbeknownst to me, I was baptized once—
a long time ago when I was a boy
and took to Earth like a hatchling to sea.

In those years, I wandered; mother too poor
and busy with maid work to keep me home,
and I, unable to take my world as it was.

My rebellious and wandering ways took me
to a congregation in worship,
spending their weekend in dance and prayer.

When I saw them huddled in a circle,
blue robes tethered to their bodies by string
and sash as they swayed around and around

the circle, the cadence roped to the blast
of a whistle that would not let them breathe,
I had to join. Through the entire night,

the congregation sang and danced
around that circle, sweat flew across the room
and fell on our dazed faces like raindrops.

The spirit came, and they shuddered and jerked,
clinging to each other's robes and fingers
as the small room sped up. Later, I fell

asleep until morning when a woman
woke me up to join the congregation on
their pilgrimage to sea. At sea, tides

roared, rolled, and curled the earth into itself.
A few priests, men of the white cloth,
stood in the sea and waited for people to wade

to them so they could give them the water.
On the beach, the lame, the sick, the poor, the mad,
stood resolute in the cold wind, waiting.

I was in the throng of the crowd, and then
I was in the first row—soon I was next
to greet the holy water. Because I

was small, a man took me into the sea,
in the large hands of a red-eyed priest.
He took my twig neck and lowered me

in. I pinched my nose
as I braved the waters. And then the world
was quiet. I was afraid and because I

was afraid, I couldn't think to flee. The priest
pulled me out of the cold water. Above the water,
the sea was an iron blanket against my chest.

The priest gripped my neck hard again
and dipped me once more. When he was done,
a church escort took me to shore

to join the sanctified shivering in wetness
and wind. Among the unsanctified, a woman
I knew in good years, here in hope that seawater

would cleanse her soul's sins and return her
to herself, tottered along the beach, muttering
to the sea, plucking the hair off her dry scalp.

I AM SUDAN

"I saw Sudan for the first time in 2009 at the Dvůr Králové Zoo in Czechia (the Czech Republic). I can recall the exact moment. Surrounded by snow in his brick and iron enclosure, Sudan was being crate trained—learning to walk into the giant box that would carry him almost 4,000 miles south to Kenya. He moved slowly, cautiously. He took time to sniff the snow. He was gentle, hulking, otherworldly. I knew I was in the presence of an ancient being, millions of years in the making (fossil records suggest that the lineage is over 50 million years old), whose kind had roamed around much of our world."

—Ami Vitale, from the October 2019 issue of National Geographic *magazine*

I was turning two
when humans came
and separated me
from my mother.

I was just beginning to learn the ways
of my kind, and the song
of the yellow-billed hornbill
and what it promised.

They chased me and my mother
with tranquilizer guns, in cars and helicopters,
threw a long thick rope
around my neck, dragged me
to my new home,
my safe space, my prison.

The humans paid my poverty-stricken guardians
irresistibly good money to hunt me down,
for they too have suffered,
enslaved, ravished,
almost extinguished, like so many
lost to Destinies Manifested,
wet dreams of the chosen ones.

I am the last,
the hope, they say,
of my kind.

You might not know it
from my gentle ways,
but in me festers rancid grief
unimaginable, grief
rich as the black soil of the Nile valley.
It burns the hopes of generations
waiting in me
to pulverized chalk.

I let this cankerous grief empty me—
no new generation will ever see
the greedy eyes of mankind, our forsaken guardian
with a sweet tooth for misery.

They try,
oh, how they try to breed me,
to make more generations of my kind
in the name of conservation.

They think they can revive us
with their tricks and sciences.
I hope they do
not succeed.

My God is death.
I wait for him
under this camel thorn tree.
A lone ring-necked mourning dove sits
on the camel thorn's grooved branch and sings
my kind's funeral dirge.

Joseph Wachira, my keeper,
is instructed to feed my syrupy longing
delicious pellets
and organic carrots
to temper human guilt;

They want me to die happy.

They think me mindless,
absent of mind,
but I know something
they don't.

A storm of their own invention is coming.

After the storm,
nothing will be left
but the tattering voice of river water
tearing the riparian fields,

no language
but the zip–zap of dragonflies in flight.

The prophecy shall be
fulfilled:
the meek shall
inherit the earth.

THERE IS NO END

to the wonders of the mind.
How a memory cuts
through a day like a rabid warthog
through a cornfield; a slanted yellow hut
bending the strict geometric shadows of city dwellings;
a pebbled escarpment tearing the present
into the valley below where I courted God
for my mother's life—
the ghost colonial brick house
where the German doctor lived half a century ago
now looming large,
sticking its gravelly elbow in my side.

And what can I glean
from places where I learned the name
of death?

Oh nostalgia! Oh hunger!

I weep for the body's departure;
how it all falls apart,
ivory after ivory after ivory.

TO THE MASTER OF SILENCE

I sense you rise
in me—
your tongue inflamed,
reddened,
and bloated with speech.

I feel your shadow
at the margins of my dreams,
hovering over my body
like a farmer inspecting
the ripeness of his fruits.

You are a thief
at three a.m. stumbling over
the fence
of my dream world
as if burdened
by a sack of secrets.

When you crawl
past the fence, your back
is a formidable wall
against my song.

You refuse to look
at my face—
Will your tongue explode?
Will our dreams burn
to smithereens if you speak?

When you unmask,
your blue eyes
are always on the floor,
swathed in shadows
like a wounded cat.

But tonight, I have left
all the lights
of my dream world on:
I am dusting every square inch
of space and time;
I am shining a bright flashlight
into your fermented silence;
I am rattling the walls
of my dreams
like a *sangoma*
beguiling the feline
and bird bones
to augur good fortune;

I have become a bat
barreling through the night,
spinning the silvery strings
of echo into music.

VILLAGE ON A MOUNTAIN, PLEASE LET ME GO

The pueblo village sits on a mountain.
The road labors slowly upward
along the steep sides of the mountain.
I can see the snow-crested peaks
of the Sangre de Cristo from the village.
It is February; a biting wind commands
the airways.

The cold adobe church
we enter feels familiar,
like my grandfather built it.

I read the dust particles of sorrow
floating about the church
like a preacher preparing a sermon.
It is as if God is pressing hard
with his index finger
on a wound I didn't know I had.

The drowsy sun beams its fragile light
through the windows of the church.

Children come out of the adobe houses
to feast on the rising sun,
as we once did
when we were children.

The children of the village have eyes
like forgotten cups of black coffee;

history and its granular residue
brew slow and calculated
in their eyes. Death billows red
in their eyes like regalia on fire.

TRANCE DANCE

In what was once a Missouri square, now a field
of primroses and clovers,
the weeping ghosts clear a circular path for me—
in the center of the circle, a small patch of yellow grass
drained by the long-drawn summer and its dawdling heat.

I lay down my oak sword on this patch,
and the four spirit doors fling open.

Above me, the clear blue sky breaks
into tears—the rain
evaporates into a cocoon of mist,
insulating me in a chorus of quakes and quivers—
I am now a perturbed pond recorrecting itself,
smoothing out its rippling ruffled feathers.

My skin tightens,
pulling closer for comfort
as the mist takes hold of me.

My teeth clench, my jaw muscles
taut
as bloodroot roots heavy with blood.

The green of the trees liquefies, joining
the distorted world whirling above my head
like dark thunderstorm clouds searching
for a common theme.

Then, the incantation.

The language I know,
they know not,
the songs I know,
they know not,
the dance I know,
they know not—but here,
in this ancient plaza of hidden mysteries,
they know it.

The old ciders know it, the strange fruiting
of black mushrooms oozing with dark secrets
and violent memories know it,
the cacti blooming yellow
among footprints of the nocturnal know it.

So, I sing and dance
and four white-tailed deer appear,
long-legged, hazelnut-eyed,
all-knowing,
yet curious
about the unraveling commotion
of booming steps and distorted faces
taking place in their field of harvest.

SONETTO AMERICANO

If I should die, in this roiling land
of blistering winters and humid heat,
my bones put to rest by ignorant hand,
form sucked by leaves of oak and sour peat
(my weary fathers, sensing the drop
of their wandering fruit, searching the dunes
of the Namib to bring their fallen crop
to lay him to rest among his kin's croon),
I say, child! Exhume those wet and rotting
bones. Take them homeward where they belong.
There, by the flocks of crowned lapwings
and the eternal refrain of their speckled song.
But if my bones to those dunes do not return,
burn them, and feed the wind that golden urn.

OUMOU SANGARÉ'S LAUGHTER

I.

Her laughter rises from the womb
Of the earth like a dust devil.
Hers is laughter honed in perennial goodbyes.
Hers is laughter that rises from the sands
Of desert(ed) landscapes. Hers is a voice that knows
Days split into pieces
Like broken calabashes.

In the sea of these historical
Dis-
Continuations,
The sea(water) up to our necks,
She laughs as though all that has been lost
Has been preserved all along,
Free and accessible as air.

II.

To the Malians
With joy,
I go. To the Malians
With joy,
I return,
To the Malians.

III.

Joy is all I remember,
When you held my hand long
And tender, like a man
Calming an orphaned fawn.
It was the way you regarded me;
I felt hefty, and present.

You reminded me of my people
From the old country,
You standing there, tall and calm,
Dark and beautiful,
Teeth white as the sheep
In Solomon's Song.

IV.

I can finally see them,
The pearls in the rain
Of Sangaré laughter,
Like the golden orbs in
And Then We Saw the Daughter
of the Minotaur!

HUMAN HISTORY

Fated to arrive
before our time, fated to go
where the dinosaurs went—
may the lesson be our salvation.

Hark! How human history unfurls
on this lonely rock, bound
to this lonely star—
the little lives we molded here,
the stories we told here,
the blood that spilled here.

Hastening to be born,
what lessons did we miss
from that primordial darkness before life,
before history?

How great we were at our height,
mighty were the stones we honed
with the hammer-edged will of our imagination;
the desserts we made out of the bitter-fleshed
seed of the pomegranate.

We arrived like a pebble cast
in the isotropic sea of the universe,
like a dense fruit
dropped prematurely.

ACKNOWLEDGMENTS

Consequence Forum: "Names and Warnings"
Doek! Literary Magazine: "*Archispirostreptus gigas*," "Dog Ode," and "Portrait of My Grandfather"
Mantis: "June Bugs," "Windeline," and "To the Master of Silence"
Quarter Press: "Bantustan Blues"
Santa Fe Literary Review: "Village on a Mountain, Please Let Me Go"
Solstice Literary Magazine: "Oumou Sangaré's Laughter"
Worcester Review: "There Is No End"